Swamps & Ponds Animal Life 2nd Grade Geography Workbook Series

Swamps and ponds are teeming
with both animal and plant life.

Frogs spend part of their lives under water and the remainder on land. A frog's skin can absorb water and helps control body temperature.

Dragonflies
are agile fliers.
The dragonfly
can hover in
mid-air. It eats
other insects,
catching them
while it is flying.

Electric eels
are capable
of generating
powerful electric
shocks of up
to 600 volts.
They inhabit
fresh waters
of the Amazon,
in floodplains,
swamps, creeks
and small rivers.

The Snail is a
soft-bodied type
of mollusk. Snails
can have lungs or
gills depending on
the species and
their habitat.

Alligator gar
are considered
euryhaline
because they can
adapt to varying
bodies of water
from freshwater
lakes and swamps
to brackish
marshes and
bays along the
Gulf of Mexico.

Alligators are reptiles. Alligator eggs become male or female depending on the temperature, male in warmer temperatures and female in cooler temperatures.

The mosquito
is a common
flying insect
that is found
around the world.
Mosquitoes
commonly infest
ponds, marshes,
swamps and
other wetland
habitats to lay
their eggs.